# Domestic Bodies

# DOMESTIC BODIES

Jennifer Ruth Jackson

Querencia Press
Chicago Illinois

QUERENCIA PRESS
© Copyright 2023

Jennifer Ruth Jackson

ISBN 978 1 959118 56 5


www.querenciapress.com


First Published in 2023

**Querencia Press, LLC**
**Chicago IL**

Printed & Bound in the United States of America

# CONTENTS

*For my husband:*

*I couldn't roll through this life without you.*
*You are my home.*

# THE PAIN OF STARTING

The hill is a cockeyed breast
Worn smooth by God & other travelers

Traversed by bicycle with bald tires
& half a deck of spoke-tickled cards

"Head straight for home," momma said
But that's a thousand miles plus

The sky bleeds past indigo, moonless
Feet slip sloppily from the pedals

"You don't need to fit in here," momma said
Palm faster than a dodge

Pointless ruminations of a youth
No concern in a rundown laundromat

Three miles away, the house waits
Clogged with tan cubes like a choked throat

# COMPARTMENTALIZATION

This is the door to your mother's voice.
Don't open it at work or ink and mascara
will smear together on your paperwork.

This is the hall that smells of her cooking.
The sound of pots and running water makes
you want to find the kitchen... and her.

This is the quilt as warm as her hug.
You wrap it around yourself as the snow
pummels windows you want to shatter.

Black lines in the newspaper reduce
her technicolor life into a logline.
You only wake to remember she's dead.

# RITUAL AT WATER'S EDGE

I watched you once, counting bones
Your breathing spaced evenly like racing hurdles
As you bound them up in cloth and rope
So we could take them to the river

The bundle made your back bend low
Your eyes could only find the soil
I cast my eyes to the sky to see the blue
Talking of clouds and bright-light things

We set the bones by the water near sunset
Washing them with coarse linen, harsh soap
You began to sing then, the soft death song
The bones hummed in response

We tossed them in like large grains of sorrowed rice
The current greedily swiped your husband's remains
Starlight found us before we reached home
I never heard your weeping above the river rush

You watched me once, after that dusk
Tears making tributaries on your sun-lined face
As the death song pulsed unwanted in my ears

Grandmother, shall I sing to your bones now?

## UNDERWATER

I drown at all the wrong moments. Places within me tighten
to fight as every spare bit of space fills up with air and anxiety.
It's a crowded room with mingling people clinking glasses on the
ocean floor. No one sees sand on their dress shoes, or that
the fluorescent bulbs are weak hints of sun-spray. We're dying
one inhale at a time as we pretend to tango, though we're
floating. We shout over the music of our own heartbeats and
watery earplugs to be heard. They laugh as bubbles form above
them. I try to escape, but I never learned how to swim.

## WATERWAY SOJOURN

Could we carve ourselves a river with
a scooped-out femur (spoon of Nile)
whitened by unabashed light?

We'd float downstream (detritus),
disinterest untethering our once-rooted
limbs from shore like trees groped by gales.

We'd make for the horizon, old friend, horizontal.
The painting with the never-captured view, framed
colors grasped on each side like a face and kissed

soundly. Swirling out. Ballerina starfish. Ears clogged.
The current will carry us, news out of print,
soggy and thinking of dry land. I never had

sea legs, legs worth seeing. Flexed feet were pretend
fins, absent of mermaid. I can't swim and am petrified
of drowning. My two-piece swimsuit a cover-up.

# HOW WE GROW UP

We skip stones on the lake, not well
Collecting them from the rubble of castle walls
Disintegrating before our eyes
Chunks *thunk* down in warning like God's wrath
Meets capital punishment for those
Inside the square, but we are not there
We dart between the largest rocks,
Abscond with the simplest prize
The stones run across the rippled sunset
Carrying away our childhood

## AFTER THE CLIMB

We lost ourselves among the leaves
falling from great heights we once knew well
branches smarting our backs Sounds of rustling
and thwacks against limbs filled the soft quiet
bruising us like rotten fruit painted in hues of dusk

# MUSCLE MEMORY

I forget wind plays rougher the faster
you run like invisible splinters tonguing
skin for entry points. I forget metal kisses

& animalistic growls by construction
sites—chewing earth with steel teeth
to force compliance. One wrong step

& you're swallowed. I forget I move
like fire with alcohol-fueled nights
in forests of old growth, burning

lush green to ash. Smoke soaking
my clothes as I undo buttons
& leave my past in the underbrush.

# SOLITARY ANIMALS

Night and every star swallowed
by a tilted moon-spoon. I'm flooded—
a plain, white woman splintered
like a reflection on stone-skipped waters.
I press you, slick to my breastbone...
translucent. We merge, oncoming traffic
the slow-motion beginning. We are
a menagerie of glass octopuses. Grace.
We travel together as once-solitary animals
near the junction of Armageddon and Wonder.

## ODE WITH ELLIPSES

I trust no other sound in my mouth…
my voice a foreign entity on the border
of my tonsil-guarded throat. I trust no
breath I feel rise hot against strands
of disobedient hair… such sighs tattle
my emotions to nearby larks. I trust only
small, rough scrapes of my teeth across
your taste buds…

## PLAY HOUSE

Tied back curtains on a kitchen stage—
peeled linoleum, apples, peals of laughter
around the rectangular table.
There is no breakfast nook, no fancy
dining room or polished silver. Everything
is dented, used—from chairs to stove.
The mother sits in a place of honor,
apron on a hook near the door
with some keys. Her plate, the only one
not sporting chips. Salsa sits in the center
of it all with unscrewed lid. Temperature
of the room pleasant enough, except when
the laughter doesn't reach the mother's eyes.

# EQUIDISTANT

Kitchen tiles mock steps untaken between us
winking clean-bright
twelve precise inches each.

In misguided symmetry, our arms fold—
a house of cards
without a pair.

We turn away, our backs closed doors.
We shut down
long ago.

Refrigerator hums a white noise dirge
to us, to love,
to that damn tile floor.

## "I'D RATHER BE DEAD
## THAN IN YOUR SHOES"

It hangs in the air between us, as though suspended
from a thousand black balloons. The scarred wood
table stretches out like my silence. He doesn't
understand what an insult it is. He can't see how much
it hurts. There is no testament to my strength, no gilded
glaze of apology. Just "fact." Just what he sees.
Just his truth. I nod, a bobblehead. Yes, I think to myself.
Yes, I know. You only see the corner of this life.
I stare down at my white sneakers, feet turned inward,
toes almost touching. He prattles on like a doll
with a perma-pulled string. There might be clarification
(understanding) in those lines of text, vibrating next
to my ears. But no. He sees me as a half-lived thing.
A caricature of all his fears. My wheelchair splashes
a boogeyman's shadow across the kitchen cabinets.

## PREPARATIONS FOR
## THE FAMILY DINNER

I strip off the green cocoon
to reveal golden studs
and slip them into salted water
like a yellow submarine

She mimics me with necessity
pulls, discards, plops
Arm muscles tense
and mouth terse

I keep to my own
feed the kettle the offerings
and pointedly ignore her set jaw

# MATRIARCHAL GENERATIONS

We walk the walk, the measured royal-reel carpet walk,
and stroll as unrolled fabric muffles footsteps.

Our mothers bake gooseberry pies with oleander crusts.
They carry serving knives in both hands behind us,

offering one little taste—a rebirth.

Our fathers meander along 25 years later, losing interest
far before the walk, stroll, unfurled, unrolled.

Though, we'd rather imagine our mothers made test pies
for them because then, it's just about us girls.

Our scepters and crowns precede us.

We learn the recipe from our mothers' toxic-sugar lips
and use whetstones on our blades until the oven timer dings.

# THE BIRD AT MY FATHER'S FUNERAL

You won't see
The blackbird with the broken wing
Driving my father's hearse
Unbandaged feathers molting from
The steering wheel
Dripping, sans ceremony, on the scythe
In the shotgun seat

I will ask
Why it is him directing death
His beak will click and snap
A cigarette worm suspiciously smelling
Of smoke-veiled soil
Like the gravediggers with ringside seats

He won't say
A syllable or caw as he stops
For the pallbearers to retrieve their burden
Marbles of midnight watch their progress

I will pilfer
His preened wing rain
And cast it onto the casket
Instead of dirt
Only shedding sorrow when
His taillights disappear

# THE FIRE

Prometheus' gift consumed my father
Belching black, flaking fragments
Into the air like confetti
Landing on my head, shoulders
As though he were blessing
Me once more

My hair remains
Unwashed

## HOW TO SURVIVE
## A COLOSSAL MISHAP

Pack a pouch of cinders from your burning house. Put it in
your purse or pocket. Spit on the ground and spin widdershins
until you feel the Earth's rotation, arms out like a sunflower
pinwheel as spikes and silk spill from your open mouth
like a wound. Kick nearby objects. Steal clouds to write
obscenities to the waning moon. Use the ashes from your ruins
to draw lines on your smoke-cured face, asemic text
no one can pronounce—your battle cry. Gather branches
and build. Roots spawn from their edges, a foundation
over the chasm of gravity on which to start again.

# DIAGNOSIS PRELUDE

1.
I'm at the edge, the Earth rendered flat by misgivings.
A mass shows on my CT scan. Sky, an abutment to our reality,
seems small. Voice of an electronic god urges me to practice Zen:
*Hold your breath.* As if I could do anything else in between tests.

2.
I yield, machinery knows me better than I do. Constellations
of my organs light up—a Simon Says game in monochrome.
A mass, where some go to pray away masses found. I haven't
seen it, my body is a city with false luminescence strong enough
to blot out stars like wine stains. Stains of red, blood, port.

3.
A signal something is *wrong*. "Wrong," a word meaning anything
from "minor" to "goodbye." I'm not prepared for any words
beyond "wait." I try to pack a suitcase in my mind's spare room,
unadorned yet scuffed. In it, I think of every dream I've ever
wanted—the few fate saw to grant, and fill it as full as I dare.

4.
I kiss his lips and smile. *It's probably nothing.* I let the whisper
drift to him as I pull him down to me, the incantation
of possibility... hope. I am paused at the edge, a fractured galaxy
of discarded moments. Another appointment tomorrow.

# REMOVAL

Black table beckons like an old car's back seat.
It is cold under spotlights for my performance
as patient number three. I ponder
frigidity and connections to the morgue.

I'm transferred, like meat on the butcher block.
Arms come out to my sides, step one of crucifixion,
a willing sacrifice. My nakedness feels foreign,
my body an empty object. To be opened,

parted, waiting for Moses in the O.R.
A mask covers my face, and I'm an astronaut
no longer considering temperature.
Space. Is. Chilly. I have no space of my own.

I wake in a different room, the room it started in.
Groundhog Day repeated, repeated except I'm sore.
I don't wish to wake and hold my breath against pain,
punishing myself by wrestling control. 75%

chance of cancer, like a meteorologist diagnosing rain.
So I'm prepared, yet not. No umbrella deflects fear.
I wait out a long weekend ceaseless, searching.
Listening for thunder coalescing with my future.

## RECURRING FEAR

It's harder than I thought, watching you watch me sicken.
An intense display of rigid muscle on offer as you cling,
whole and hale, to my arms. As if to koala-grab my soul.
I am the eucalyptus between your teeth, lost in haze.

I'll carry my flowers like on our wedding day. Chemicals
devour pages if we try to press them. God's annoyance
at diminishing the 3D world is present as I lie still. I still lie,
and say I'm not afraid of a second cancer. Like anemic luck,

we'll chase hope, but it will disappoint us the same way
a childhood favorite is ruined by adult eyes and sensibility.

# THORACOTOMY IN EDEN

Indentation in my chest, I'm sew(n) together now.
Did you see the surgeon saw my rib in half?
Where is the missing piece? Could I have a funeral
or wake of ash when not under anesthesia?

I wish I could carve runes in the bone, a story
carried deep, and summon Eve who will love me
more than Adam because I'll give her agency
and apples and all the pretty, red things I possess—

like the four-inch scar on my chest I dedicate to her.

## YOU ON THE PALATE

Let me taste you again and discover
(with this chemo mouth) what flavor
you are now that chemicals damage
my tongue and wrap it like a wetsuit.
Are you the bitterness of milk?
My new intolerance to citrus?
Will your metamorphosis please
like ice cream? Are you complementary
to my blood-weep gums? Do you still
leave the full-body twist upon my lips?
I still detect the salt you're half made of.

## AGONY AND MASS

There is nothing interesting where you are. My body
builds an empire as a dishonest queen. My body
shudders into oncoming traffic, stoplights signal,
"Go form another universe from a useless womb,"
bleeding black, thick like leeches. Reach
exhausts from such demands. Your hands slip,
rocks melt under your touch, turn to dough.
My pale, fat flesh kneaded into shapes it can't sustain,
lying about the pain it can take. Lying for us both.

## ARCHITECT OF THE THRONE

You built an empire, cradled
it in your arms. Scaffolding
sticking from the blanket until unveiling
erect structures near the heart.
Highways lead back to warehouses
where we stored our bread,
stale from open air. Your lungs

tired from billowing smoke. I sat,
reclined, listening to your story come
to life in the harbor of your chest. And I,
with such curious, exquisite fingers,
chased birds around your crown,
grazing the tallest skyscrapers
until your sighs heralded the dawn.

## UNREPENTANT

We hug—squeeze & hiss air like empty ketchup
bottles clutched in sweat-moistened fists. Like cash,
we wear green & security strips with our swirls.

Do you practice palmistry? See our heart lines there?
(Dried rivers that kiss & carry us when we pray.)
Entwine our fingers, gnarled with arthritic roots,
in a dime-store imitation of affection. Our voices, slick
affectations, recite hymns with sewn lips in fields

our fathers tend. We wilt under their sun-dried eyes
as angels descend like pigeons, gluttonous & cooing,
for the discarded crumbs of our atonement.

# PRICKLES

There is a bit of love in the body.
Thistles down your throat (sideways)
scratch the esophagus in infatuation.

It hurts you to breathe. Hyper-aware of air—
the push, pull, and flow of every molecule
lost to look, thought, or touch.

A submission sans silk rope. Purple
flowers float along inside your stomach
with blood-glazed, open petals.

# DROWNED, CARVED STONES

We were stone frogs in the bathtub
Eroding our noses for air, a glimpse
Of mint lily pad over the lip
Jump, it's futile now, as it was then
I shouldn't have minded when
You tucked legs under and used me
To spring upon, your underwater diving
Board in bids for freedom
We didn't hold chips for, but the salt
Such generous pinches, the day
Your languid tongue slicked beyond
A princess' mouth, cast you an emerald
Coat—I wait in the wet of sorrow
Praying for rain

## REFLECTION ON
## THE MORTALITY OF BEASTS

"There is a horse in the water,"
that is how you say it,
no matter if the animal is brown
or mare or stallion.

You vaguely wonder how long
it can swim—can it even?

How impossibly large the lake seems
with silver waves etched,
almost stunning,
sunlight visibly tittering at its reflection.

*Not so beautiful to the horse,* you think
but do not say, to the old woman made
of leather and scarves to your right.

Your hand is to your ashen lips while men
plunge like doctors' needles
into the water and swim out, trying to reach
the island of head and plastered mane.

It dips under, your breath
catches in sympathy or fear and you
wait, chastising the waves for being.

The men paddle slowly back
to shore, one gently cradling
a dripping, dark brown bridle in an arm
as if the horse's spirit followed.

# CAPSIZE

We wait for the ferry at midnight
Wind bends our backs like grass
For the red-nosed operator
We genuflect beneath the clouds
Like waves against the dock
(Bass notes of the boat's horn)
Filled with tremors and doubt

With thirteen stones in our pockets
(Exact change cupped in our palms)
Night drinks the land before us
Moonbeams splash on our faces
Blessings of a sun-forsaken god
Shuffle us forward with suitcases
As opaque as the black water

# GRIEF TICKLES LIKE A HAMMER

Our wits had fled
on tiptoe.
It was morning,

though, the butterscotch
sun swirled among
clouds, when we

first noticed. Pain splashed
vibrant and ugly,
a Christmas sweater of black

cats. It was spring.
Not like now, winter's bite
leaves teeth marks

on our bones. We bang
our heads and search
scrambled brains.

We remember meeting you,
the synapse-snap
audible, pleasant,

like castanets and margaritas
trickling onto tongues, into ears.
You were worth it

to us.

# RITE OF PASSAGE

Your father will take you out today
Aiming won't be the hardest part
(metallic jolt in hands and mind)
you shy away from his touch
but it won't help you escape
inside camouflage and foliage
You will never leave the woods

to shoot a gun for the first time
you have to deal with the kickback
When dad says you'll kill sometimes
He means to comfort you
The rabbit-like part of you screams
against the reality of a forest
innocent and ignorant of the future

## ABSENTEE FATHER

Pause, cut the applause off mid-cheer
And screams mid-screech like a bird of prey
Strangled in flight, body never found,
Never touching down

Erase the players off the grass, scrub them
With the brush of age or sponge of amnesia
Light uniforms (dandelion puffs) sift breezes during drifts

Ignore the sore limbs body-promised
By unyielding plank seats
Our shifting (no relief) frozen with the spectators now
Your head bowed as though you seek
Removal from this snapshot of time

## LIGNIN

I watched the yellowing of pages
(your journals) each individual
leaf sick, so unlike daffodils
(your favorite).
I know.
Illness is better than the dead
of bone-white shuffled by fingers
mourning your hair. At least
recovery is still a dream...
sufficient.

## PLAGUES OF EGYPT

She sustained the boils without a whimper
Slept next to rotting, bloated frog bodies
Consumed flies and locusts in her dreams
Rinsed her mouth with muddy water
After the Nile turned as red
As the welts raised by clomping hail

But three days of fiery darkness
Lit fear like a lantern
Whispers of the final plague
Reached her like a slap

And when it came to her doorstep found
No sons, nor daughters, and passed her by
They slept eternally at her side
As she watched it pass, poisoned cup to her lips

# WINGED MONARCH

My son, my sun, fly towards
a moon brighter than cat eyes
peering from the dark, grab
angel wings like a devil
denied so long those delicate,
delicious features.

Clouds will be your sign of royalty,
the crown upon your
heathen brow upheld, as flighty
subjects honk your praise
and name. It was your father's,
slip into it like a shirt.

Ground left bereft of you will never
kiss your soles again, as you
are blessed. Blue, weighted sky above
will just crack open, an Easter
egg with a yolk of stars and
night to be devoured.

Will you remember your mother up
there when her hair tickles
your back as knotted rope?
When you stretch my dress and flesh
to soar and bones to steer?
Will you, at least, cry for me when it rains?

# SEVERING SCARS

We are interchangeable, have no names, as we struggle
in the cocoon created by mother's arms.
She repeats the adage of oppression strengthening
and plants the pinprick razors in our backs, already
slick with sweat, now blood, too.

Her tuneless hum hammers into our skulls, guiding
the journey carved into our flesh as she describes our wings
in the firelight (supposedly tucked softly by her elbows).
Our heads, resting near mother's own scars and flightless form
nod, never believing we'd someday mimic the path of pain
upon our trusting daughters.

# TAILLIGHTS

You skitter, fluff like goose down... down a highway
sewn with paint. Cars see the uneven stitching.

Yellow and vulgar, lurid in sunlight. Moonlight-headlights

cut like white stripes near the shoulders. A country road's
spaghetti-strap dress. Necessary without air

conditioning in humid heat. You can't go home again.

Wheels faster than feet kick and crunch and ignore...
like you wish you could. You would, if things were different.

Gasp as though one good kiss of oxygen might spare you

from looking back. Rust-flakes tremble off the truck.
Objects in mirror are closer than they appear.

## THOSE WHO INHERIT

Come, hungry hippos, another of your rank has died!
Set the table with napkins of will and testament. Slam
open your mouths to feast. White marbles morph

to diamonds in gold settings. Morsels become parcels
of property. Bare your teeth and gaping maws
at your brethren in wordless shrieks of gluttony.

Attend your corners in petulance and consume
possessions acquired by one you loved—one whose
name your lips cannot form while they await another bite.

## BANDANAS

My grandfather carried a cross with him
on his forehead—a small, green tattoo
he covered with bandanas while he worked.
"Don't let no one see that," his boss said,
as grandpa tapped his lettered-up knuckles
on the guest chair. "We are a Christian nation."
Maybe there are only certain ways to show
love as an ex-con where ex is debatable
like politics at Thanksgiving. Maybe it was better
to cover God's eyes as he drank Him away.

## IF ONLY I'D SPOKEN TO THE GOD
## IN MY REARVIEW MIRROR

Dionysus dunks stretched vines in silver, twists them
into wreaths, crowns hares near the columns by my driveway.
My windshield sheds prickly leaves, flora tears forgotten in eastern
gusts. The gas pedal shrinks against my foot, succumbs to pressure.
Houses whip by on a carousel reel—street names more foreign
than Mars' soil. My neck will not oblige a look back, locked by stress
like my driver side door. Sun slices into my eyes (royal gold).
On some distant hill, better days appear. I thumb creases in my toga
at a stoplight, searching for an answer beyond "no." The God raises
his glass in salute or for a refill.

# TELEVANGELIST

Greasy cash beneath hot lights
Slimy palms pressed to bodies, heads
Shiny hallelujah Rolex

Inoperable cancers
Aluminum walkers, canes
Our deaf and our blind

How much money per miracle?

# THE WORD IS "DISABLED"

Yes, I am *that cripple* with callused
knees and suede-soft soles,

with two focused eyes, though only
one can be steered straight at a time.

I am *that gimp* you give glares to like candy
when you ram your cart into me. My fault?

For existing, I pay a higher tax than you.
Stairs keep me out of businesses more than locks.

I am *that wheelchair*, no name or gender
when you talk about the space I take

that you could have. Any I take is too much.
Anything I need is labelled opulence overlap.

All decadence. *That handicapped woman.*
Who dares to breathe, laugh, fuck on your watch?

My life should be misery to you. Until I die,
who else could make your life seem blessed?

I am *that leech* you accuse of bankrupting your country.
Yours. Like it isn't also mine. Like I can love it, but

it can't reciprocate, embrace my twisted limbs.
Pat the bed beside itself and promise to care forever.

# BEDBOUND

A film of soreness settles onto my skin (absorbs) reels into my
neck and head. I watch fan blades blur into the ceiling as ache
arches through my system. I'm having a dream of agony
with open eyes and clenched teeth. My body mingles with
my sheets and leaves impressions. Leaves outside my window
are falling, falling. Sky crashes through my roof and dances
on my scalp. Me, Atlas-hat askew, avoids the glare of sunlight
heating my angry bones like copper coils. Chronic: this pain-filled
horizon is forever. I bury myself in piles of blankets and scream
for release until a flock of mother birds alight on a power line
across the street and sing me into uneasy rest. Winged notes
carry me from myself.

## FOLLOW THE LIGHT

I track it with my eyes. No head turn allowed. My neck locks
like a gate I'm scared to open. Do it only the way the doctors say.
It must be correct. There is a sequence. They are not dancing.

I self-deprecate. It's a form of self-destruction. I can disarm
them if I aim the gun at myself, if I pull the trigger first. I do.
They laugh like they deserve to. I laugh like I must. Recoil jolts

through my body. The lens is difficult for them. Crip forms
are foreign. I'm megafauna on wheels, familiar but unidentified
in their country of waiting rooms. I'm a galaxy removed

from anything they see as human. My bones are all there, minus
a few inches of rib. Organs exist in correct orbit to others
of my species. Bullets of self-barbs at the ready.

# YOU WANT ME (TO PERFORM PAIN)

Would you like me to stick a knife
into the butcher block of my trauma,
make it bleed a little onto the page:
A pulp stage of tearstained performance,
spotlight on my mouth open wide
in an anguish aria? Would you close curtains
on this smile to quietly peek behind once
a sob seeps through? Do I pantomime
pain for you, hiding love in my arteries
like a form of cholesterol that's just as deadly
but not shown on the 6:00 news?

## TARGET AUDIENCE

The roles made from my people
torn from our lives, chrome,
and chronic skin neglect us
on the reel. Be real, it's not
to honor us or hold us up
like bearing walls. It's mimic,
it's removed and remade
palatable for a viewership
where we are scrubbed glossy
with Photoshop. We can't tell
our stories without their hands
on our cracking, dislocated jaws.

## THE YEAR IS A CENTURY

I'm too furious to be still tonight.
Twitter feuds clog my mentions, please
keep my name away from your auto-
complete. Newscasters solemn between

political vitriol. Natural disasters in unnatural
hues. Drumbeat storms and combat marches
blast out of my satellite radio like the bombs
we think of dropping. Another death down

the block. We got too close again, Icarus,
to other humans with pulled-tight smiles
we aren't supposed to see. Shortages come,
the new thing we didn't realize was important

disappears—another notch in our civility.
I was once asked to be kind to a eugenicist
arguing against my cripple-life. Put the mask on,
swallow bile like cyanide. Too furious to be still,

I scream and shake with a night on fire.

## UPDATE

There's a ticker tape across my teeth
shouting with its blue & white
the words I hum behind pursed lips
like regurgitated subway tokens. I take
the stairs because I'm a thief, unable
to traverse or ride the rail below, feet
engaged in a stomp-dance of rights
mashed best between the toes of those
with $200 pedicures. Ooze is their shine,
polished blessings of quarters flicked
at a homeless person & called "charity."

## MR. DICTIONARY

The only passive noun in a masculine language is "woman." First
syllable as gentle apology, not clarification as in "human." It is
a soft, pliant word like "womb" or "thigh." It is a delicate word
like "embroidery." Whoa, man! Do you really respect that
person? Whoa, man. Do you really see her as an equal? Whoa,
man. Whoa. It's a hysterical word, a wild animal tumbling about
in a dress and killer heels. It is a timid mouse, a cunning shrew,
a fat whale. It is an othered word, mysterious. Don't try
to connect or understand. Let it bend around your parted teeth,
submissive.

## POEM FOR MY MOTHER

I ask when I'll see you again, but you're quiet.
My lips can't stop forming syllables that quiver
like a let-go spring, an alarm to your silence.
You've never not answered me before.
Each night, I speak to any god about your absence,
not knowing if they hear me. If they do, I'd know
you might. I hate talking to my ceiling
about how much I miss you and pretending
it's heaven—that you're there, above me,
an arm's length away beyond the sun.

## DISENCHANTMENT MASK

I fade, sucked inside a floral-print dress stacked
with violets I'm allergic to, scooping sand into my head…
my feet glued inside sky-high heels.

I paint my face, lipstick clownish, red and wall-thick.
It gives me space between teeth and kisses...
sharp, popped heat like forge-bright needles.

I am this doll of cracked, aged porcelain (covered
with mothball scent) you take from a different
space than where you place your love.

If I yell my name, will you know me better then?
My mouth shudders with the pain of knowing only words
you cram in there. I, sucked inside, fade.

# THEMED HOTEL ON ASPEN STREET

I am the cracked, crystal woman in The Bison Room,
my imprint on the carpet in a ring of sand. I slough
off a cloak of filtered light, swallow iridescence like scarabs—
legs inside my throat and lungs. A clock on the bedside table
trills out in alarm. Your sleep-heavy hand falls, misses,
rises again to strike home. Slaps often proceed
silence, I know. More with you than anyone.

Fissures (decorative, you say) tattoo me until I chip.
I'm messy. You clear away pieces—a champagne flute
knocked over in a passion fit. I wonder if you throw
them out, the frosted parts held by ghost-tape
and stale smoke. If they ever cut you.
If you ever shine them, your prismatic trophies,
coating you in rainbows as you pour more sand.

# REFRACTORY GRAINS

Who am I when not consumed? My flesh adorned
with pearls of residual teeth marks is filled with longing.

Minnows swim in my belly like an unheated cauldron. Phantom
fire stalls in my chest—a distant threat of torch-bright breath.

My fingers tap my cellphone out of sleep, rest is a toil-worn beast
of mottled fur and fangs. Digital pattern brings your voice through

satellites—bowls large enough to slip inside while you tear into me.
Each slow-chewed morsel more of you as I transform into stardust.

## ANOTHER FAILED LDR

I taste him in your mouth, his name stretched
past three syllables on your frosted tongue.
Combination of lime & taffy dreams. Lipstick

on your teeth like perfumed blood. Kiss goodbye
blotted on the bathroom mirror. You hold
phones in place of babies & beaus. Condensed

love pressed to your ear like a conch shell.
It isn't waves you long to hear anymore,
but merry message-chimes. Acronyms

absorbed into your workday. I'm shocked to hear
him in your voice, your disconnected overage,
the lack of hang-ups as you brush my gums

in your need to feel something IRL.
We all sound the same in text form. You won't
even need to close your eyes & pretend.

# THE NIGHT HE CHEATS

She walks trenches into the floor
Polished, three inches deep
A dry river flowing her between rooms
Vinyl rasps from the bedroom as the needle
Skips, skips, skips
The death rattle after a single melody
On an old 45 RPM record
His well-oiled .22 Luger balances out
A cigarette hemorrhaging ash
Filter pressed to a bottle of Johnnie Walker Red
Wearing mauve lipstick around the rim

## BIBLIOPHILE

Once I held the heart of a paper man
crumpled like dreams in my palm.
Corrective ink glazed four fingers
as they brushed fluttering ventricles,
each feeble beat a rustle of pages
near the end of a book.

Speech bubbles on graphic display,
holes punched in him clear to the spine.
Reshelve or recycle his feelings gone
to pulp? I can't read him, anymore.
Our romance, rebranded a murder
mystery, teems with rust-hued herring.

# THE MEANING OF BIBLIOMANCY

We crack spines, easy as eggs, and point to random definitions
in the dictionary—ask for correlations between Latin roots
and Greek. Keys to express our disordered selves wind
through passages of The Odyssey. Our love discomfited
with accusing jabs at Jane Eyre. E-readers (ineffective)

keep turning our pages onwards... futures lost
in half-deciphered prose. We fear probes and prods
of slick, slimy poetry that won't tell us truth
since everything possible is negotiable and slant
between stanzas. A comma is a pause or itself an end.

# HONEY

Collect and leave me raw at the bottom
of a bottle—my unhinged jaw in a jar
stamped with wild blackberries. Filter out
bodies like a Vogue double-issue. Let me
pour, thick and sweet, into your throat
as I coagulate. Pick your teeth
with my comb until it twangs and moves
along your gums—a slight sting to call
the blood. Your name raises hives along
my arms. Drone on as I hasten the swarm.

# UNOBSTRUCTED VIEW

Since you're not yet a soldier,
shed the camo from your thoughts
and sit with me, at ease.

Branches above are not helicopter blades,
the only whistles are from birds, not bombs.

A swiveling head won't increase survival here.
The man with the gun is a citizen, sans target.

Sniff the wind deep, free of sand, and let your mind
drift past doorways you have known
where no enemies hide.

Swig champagne after the *pop* and not lose your cool.
This is the last gift I can give, the wish you never uttered, granted.

Sit and keep this memory with you—the way the world was.

# TYRANNY

We don't give the "Top Man" more power
than he ought to have, armed guards do that well enough.
Brown and crimson-clad soldiers flood the streets
like overflowed sewage, making it unsafe to walk.

Guns, large and numerous, are the discount toys of our lord.
Who will fight back when the night smells of blood
and gunpowder when they are merciful,
when a knife is our best weapon to his grenade?

We fade like flowers in winter, hoping we're hidden
below the teeth of salt. For us women, they save
worse fates than bullets, generally quick,
not granted to us despite our monsoons of tears.

## CASUALTIES

We held, at first, the line
Then, when it broke, each other
Whistles (artillery) our lullaby
Booming impact, our "Reveille"
We can still smell flesh (human)
Within the crater, once our country

## SACRAMENT OF LOSS

Your heart, resting on a wooden staircase,
   is squished with splinters in all ventricles.
      Blood smears track the second it was lost,
         tumbled free like it wrestled with the dryer's
            highest cycle. You are used to bleach, caustic
               and holy. No hand wash, a sign of the cross
                  on Sunday. Hole in your chest, a silent sermon.

## I'M A GHOST, MYSELF

Who hasn't died in public once? A tail
of toilet paper or false bravado follows
you out of the conference room like a puppy.
A piano falls on you from the height of scorn
as aloft as your mother-in-law's nose.
Who hasn't wilted under chipped facades
made easier to plaster over with masks sold
at every corner store? Who hasn't professed
love to the silence beyond a sigh? We are
sterile phantoms who gain reincarnation
through coffee and selective memory,
retail therapy and social media.

## EDIBLE BLOSSOMS

I bring you fragrant flowers—large blooms
collapsed against slender stem-necks

so you may run them delicately through
dainty, wood-chipper teeth. Perfume dribbles

from your eyes, and I bottle it like hair color.
Peroxide blond a lie—a nectar of aspartame.

Drink and wear your over-processed bounty.
Slather it between your toes while I gather

baskets for our walk—packing bouquets
like stacks of logs in case you wish to cry.

# MISDIRECTION

Bags breeze past my ankles in an empty lot,
the twisted heads of plastic ghosts.
Not a lot can happen here, except everything.
Accept it, I'm lost loading Google Maps in 2015.
It's too far to walk, though civilization is everywhere
like hives. My skin reddens from the cold.

I am Santa Claus planning retirement.
I am Amelia Earhart flying towards grave adventure.
I am the Bermuda Triangle swallowing sailors.

On a street corner, I turn left. It's never right.
It doesn't stop me, though my phone gets no signal.
Not so smart in Nowhere Land, like government
SafeThink and GroupThink and man, at least a hive
mind has honey and directions. Security, however
false, is something cultivated. Fabrication allows me
enough room to shove off, get lost.

I am Columbus without the genocide.
I am a Salem Witch without the burn.
I am a misplaced woman without a clue.

No one to take me in, no hotel or inn to keep me.
Few hostels in this country, people too hostile
to share space. Am I a grounded astronaut?
Will the stars guide me home? There
is a Starbucks on every corner bankrupting
me with twenty-ingredient concoctions. Is someone
better searching this grid of concrete and road signs?
Will they look for me between cappuccinos?

I miss 8-track tapes I haven't seen in person.
I miss the absence of self-realization.
I miss the turn near my apartment every day.

# EXTRAVAGANCE

i taste live flesh
dancin' in a suit not me
baggy, bawdy, there

a puffed-up, bloated phoenix
molted lava pourin' down
my feathers rain twice

dizzy, Death stops its pace
i give bags to the hangman
once more, to the compost heap

i burn in lieu of decay

# TO THE NINES

Bring out the diamonds
splayed like a fan or legs
akimbo, sequenced from least
to most. Surprise escalation
drips over the table as talk

trickles in champagne tickles.
Pick out the number you favor
and gods smile at your superstition
as you slide it to someone
on your left. Pocket the rest

like loose change and hope
for fate to fall into you. Wait
for fortune to call your name
at the last telephone booth
in all of America. Scatter

your last few chips among
elderly women smoking
by the slots and head for home
to the welcome ring of raining
quarters and nickels. Closer moons.

# ELEGY FOR MY SANITY

I wonder where you go when you aren't with me,
clicking and plinking as rain from a slot machine.

Do you even know, or do you slip between
couch cushion sewer grates and into darkness?

Would you tell me if you knew?

An elephant strolls away with my skin
and you play games.

Did you send it? The message spelled out in loose
buttons that rattle like my teeth?

I watch them roll out of reach
(buttons or teeth, I'm not sure which).

My fingered hands form a cage to catch you.

I just want to talk to you about the striped,
singing owl in my shower.

## CAPRICORN & CANCER

I want to dive into your cherry
eyes & pluck the pits for coffee
I can drown in. You swivel
in your cheapest suit, jacket
left crumpled near a pillow

like a candy wrapper. I wait
for you to say what I know
is coming, truth harder to cough
out when the only brew in this two
-star hotel is cold & decaffeinated.

## ASTRONOMY IN TIME

We constructed a new moon
with half-empty wine bottles
and half-dead stars. Gazers,
we rested our backs on a hill
darker than the sky in its navy
blazer. You were my Copernicus
and I your Galileo—all bright
theories and significance.
We cut slices of the universe
and fed each other, grasping
cosmos and hands decades apart.

# SPLASHES OF COLOR

Paint oozes between my toes. My soles are brushes
of stained-glass light, floorboards—warm canvas
I trod across, leaving prints. Lines and crevices
my signature. I move through rooms marking doorways
with powder blue. Skip to the kitchen in spring-green
joy. Slide stripes of navy along corners of my bedroom,
streaks from my heels once decorated sheets and his thighs.
Lilac splatters leave a trail to the patio and fade away.

# FUNERAL WEATHER

morning breaks, just like me
wearing blue on its edges
until it expands & drenches
the sky

## QUALITATIVE HUMANITY

We are coins with denominational
differences. The few eroded by time
& rough landings. The kind worried
by warm thumbs in thin pockets.
Bicentennials lost down sewer
grates, both special & forgotten.
The commemorative quarters
of her birth state in an ashtray,
her last reminder of home.

## MY FINAL FAREWELL

Set me adrift, rocked in my eternal sleep
by shushing waves. Let the sun dip
and stars dance as flame-tipped arrows
from the shaking bows of those I love
streak towards me like mini comets,
tears adding more salt to the sea.
My pyre lighting up the water
as a contradiction of elements.
Maybe, as the sand cradles their feet,
I'll hear them singing—cracking
voices raised in unison one more time
for me like a birthday song. The largest
candle extinguishing with my last wish.

# INDIVIDUAL
# ACKNOWLEDGEMENTS

Momma, you always encouraged me to write, even when you didn't want to read a word I wrote. I know this isn't the book that will make me the female Stephen King, but I hope you'd be proud. I miss you every day.

Gene, thank you for being the best big brother you know how to be. You're smarter than you know.

Tony, your philosophies helped shape what I believe. You left us too soon.

Morley, thank you for inspiring my art with your own. I can't wait to see you grab the art world by the throat.

Susan, heart-sister, I learn perseverance and grace by watching you. You are more talented than I'll ever be.

Dad and Mom Jackson, thank you for always treating me like family. You are #RelationshipGoals.

Marie, you teach me about the subtle gifts of daily life. I hope to age as gracefully as you.

Lisa Reynolds, your poetry is beauty in brevity. Our correspondence is something I cherish.

F.I. Goldhaber, you are a kick in the pants of life. You force me to reevaluate the world and myself frequently.

Su Zi, you are a renaissance woman. I learn so much from you.

Mrs. Anderson from Mattoon Elementary School, you are the reason I started writing.

Disability activists, thank you for fighting for our community. Your work allows me to do mine.

Dear readers, I appreciate you so much! I hope you're able to connect with at least one of the poems in this collection. If so, I'll have done my job.

# ACKNOWLEDGEMENT OF
# FIRST PUBLICATION

"The Pain of Starting" was published in *Red Earth Review*

"Ritual at Water's Edge" won third place in the Balticon Poetry Contest in 2014

"Waterway Sojourn" was published in *Arlijo*

"How We Grow Up" was published in *Thimble Literary Magazine*

"After the Climb" was published by *Fragmented Voices*

"How to Survive a Colossal Mishap" and "'I'd Rather be Dead Than in Your Shoes'" were published in issue four of *Snarl*

"The Bird at My Father's Funeral" and "Elegy for My Sanity" were published in *Brine Literary*

"Diagnosis Prelude" was published in *Bacopa Literary Review*

"Thoracotomy in Eden" and "Bedbound" were published in *Blanket Sea*

"Target Audience" and "You on the Palate" were published in *Rabid Oak*

"Agony and Mass" was published by *South Florida Poetry Journal*

"Reflection on the Mortality of Beasts" was published in *Banshee* (issue four)

"Capsize" was published in *Otis Nebula*

"Grief Tickles like a Hammer" was first published in *Sparks of Calliope*

"Rite of Passage" was published by *Tilted House*

"Plagues of Egypt" was published by *Wild Age Press* on September 22nd, 2015

"Winged Monarch" was published in *Polu Texni* on June 27th, 2016

"Severing Scars" was published in *Altered Reality Magazine*

"The Word is 'Disabled'" is forthcoming in *Concrete Desert Review*

"Another Failed LDR" was published by *Furious Gazelle*

"The Night He Cheats" was published in *Algebra of Owls*

"Bibliophile" was published in *FERAL: A Journal of Poetry & Art*

"Misdirection" was published by *Vinyl Poetry* on March 6th, 2019

"Astronomy in Time" first appeared in *Tipton Poetry Journal*

"Qualitative Humanity" was published in *little somethings press*

"My Final Farewell" was published in *Rudderless Mariner Poetry*

Printed in the USA
CPSIA information can be obtained
at www.ICGtesting.com
LVHW090604261123
764808LV00067B/2542